Fine Art Studio

Drawing

by Jim Bradrick

ARTIST'S ERASER
VITAGUM
DRY CLEANER

For My Wife, Joni

Silver Dolphin

Silver Dolphin Books
An imprint of the Advantage Publishers Group
5880 Oberlin Drive, San Diego, CA 92121-4794
www.silverdolphinbooks.com

Fine Art Studio: Drawing is produced by becker&mayer!,
Bellevue, Washington
www.beckermayer.com

If you have questions or comments about this product, send e-mail to
infobm@beckermayer.com

ISBN-13 : 978-1-59223-327-4
ISBN-10 : 1-59223-327-9

Produced, manufactured, and assembled in China.

7 8 9 10 09 08 07

06389

Edited by Betsy Henry Pringle
Written and illustrated by Jim Bradrick
Art direction by J. Max Steinmetz
Designed by Eddee Helms and J. Max Steinmetz
Design assistance by Karrie Lee
Packaging design by Scott Westgard
Product development by Lillis Taylor
Production management by Katie Stephens

Image Credits

Every effort has been made to correctly attribute all the material reproduced in
this book. We will be happy to correct any errors in future editions.

Page 3: Cave painting of horses courtesy of and document elaborated
with the support of the French Ministry of Culture and Communication,
Regional Direction for Cultural Affairs–Rhône-Alpes, Regional Department of
Archaeology.

Page 4: Pablo Picasso, *Mother and Child* and *Maternity with a Red Curtain*,
© 2004 Estate of Pablo Picasso / Artists Rights Society (ARS), New York, photo
credit: Scala/Art Resource, NY. Used with permission.

Page 7:
Michelangelo Buonarroti, *Study for the Head of Leda*, photo credit: Scala / Art
Resource, NY. Used with permission.

Page 9: Wayne Thiebaud, *Around the Cake*, Spencer Museum of Art, University
of Kansas, Gift of Ralph T. Coe in memory of Helen F. Spencer. Used with
permission.

Page 10: Bas-relief showing a pharaoh from the Temple of Horus in Edfu,
photo © Alfred Molon. Used with permission.

Page 12: Henri Matisse, *Still Life with Apples on a Pink Tablecloth,*
© 2004 Succession H. Matisse, Paris / Artists Rights Society (ARS),
New York, image © Board of Trustees, National Gallery of Art,
Washington, D.C. Used with permission.

Page 22: Vincent van Gogh, *The Cafe Terrace on the Place du Forum,
Arles, at Night,* photo credit: Erich Lessing / Art Resource, NY. Used
with permission.

Page 23: Vincent van Gogh, *Fishing Boats on the Beach at Saintes-
Maries,* photo credit: Snark / Art Resource, NY. Used with permission.

Page 28: Dante Gabriel Rossetti, *La Ghirlandata,* photo credit: Erich
Lessing / Art Resource, NY. Used with permission.

Page 32: James McNeill Whistler, *Symphony in White, No. 1: The
White Girl,* image © 2004 Board of Trustees, National Gallery of Art,
Washington, D.C. Used with permission.

Page 34: Salvador Dalí, *The Persistence of Memory,* © 2004 Salvador
Dalí, Gala-Salvador Dalí Foundation / Artists Rights Society (ARS),
New York, photo credit: Digital Image © The Museum of Modern
Art / Licensed by Scala/Art Resource, NY. Used with permission.

Page 40: Cave painting of bison courtesy of and document
elaborated with the support of the French Ministry of Culture
and Communication, Regional Direction for Cultural Affairs—
Rhône-Alpes, Regional Department of Archaeology; Bas-relief,
Michelangelo, Vincent van Gogh, Henri Matisse, and Salvador Dalí
images are credited above.

The Man in the Moon

What do you suppose was the first drawing—the very first? You have to imagine a time when there were no pencils, no paper, and no stores selling art supplies. You have to imagine a time before written language, because the first letterforms were simple drawings. You have to go back even before the first time a hunter picked up a stick and drew in the dust to show where the antelope were grazing.

Perhaps the idea for the first drawing came from nature. It might have been the man in the moon.

When you look up at the full moon in the night sky, do you see a face there? Most everyone sees some kind of image—an image that is not even really there! (When we look at the moon enlarged with lenses, we see only craters.)

It is the human need to look for patterns and meaning in things that makes it possible for you to see a human face on the face of the moon, and it is the imagination of humankind that enables us to look at marks on a canvas or a piece of paper and see a mountain, a city, or a person. The first drawing may have been natural, yet it wasn't long before someone—perhaps some girl or boy—made a drawing on purpose.

The people who looked at it and saw what the artist intended for them to see must have been amazed. It must have seemed like magic.

Even now, in our age of telescopes and digital photographs, the magic is still there. It is the magic of drawing.

What Is Drawing?

Drawing is making lines on a surface to show or depict something. Most drawings are created on paper, but you can also find them on the canvas of a painting, on pottery, and even on stone.

Although drawings are often black lines on white paper, they can be any combination of tones and colors.

How is drawing different from painting?

Sometimes it is hard to say. Most painting includes some drawing.

Pablo Picasso, *Maternity with a Red Curtain*, 1922. Oil on canvas, private collection.

Pablo Picasso, *Mother and Child*, 1922. Pen and ink drawing, Coll. Picasso, Mougins, France.

Virtuoso Picasso

Pablo Picasso (1881–1973) painted in many different styles in his lifetime, but most of them began with strong drawing. Picasso had his first art exhibition at the age of thirteen.

Although he was only five feet two inches tall, Picasso is one of the biggest art figures of the twentieth century. He was a sculptor, graphic artist, and ceramicist, but he is best known for his paintings and for the creativity he brought to all his artwork.

DID YOU KNOW?
When Picasso was a little boy in Spain, he would bring a pigeon to school and spend his time drawing the pigeon instead of doing his schoolwork.

Often, a drawing is a finished work of art in itself, but it may also be a means to an end, like the sculptor's drawing of the statue he will carve.

"Every child is an artist. The problem is how to remain an artist once we grow up."
—Pablo Picasso

Sometimes a drawing is not intended to be art at all, but only information, like the map to your house you make for a friend.

Learning to put in the right information so that the viewer sees what you want is what drawing is all about.

In fact, information is what every drawing contains. Maybe this is a good way to think about drawing. A portrait that is a good likeness of its subject carries the information of what that subject looks like to anyone who sees the portrait.

If you love to draw, then you will spend a lifetime learning more and more about what to put in and what to leave out. No drawing book can teach you everything you need to know, and anyway, most of your learning can come only from practice.

But perhaps this book can get you started in a good way.

The Artist's Tools

These fine art tools are included in your kit. Here's what they are for:

Graphite Pencils

The soft pencil (4B) makes the blackest line, but its softness also means that it will not hold a sharp point. Use it for bold drawings and for shading.

The hard pencil (2H) holds a sharp point and makes a faint gray line. Use this pencil for your beginning, or preliminary, drawings and for very precise drawing.

The medium pencil (F) is in between the other two in both hardness and darkness.

Artist's Mannequin

Pose the mannequin to draw realistic human figures, cartoon characters, monsters, or anything else that stands on two feet like a person.

Sketchbook

Carry your sketchbook with you to draw on the bus, at the mall, or at the beach.

White Pencil

Use the white pencil to create highlights or bright areas in a drawing done with dark lines, or to make a drawing of white lines on colored paper.

Paper

This book comes with ten sheets of paper in different colors. For your practice, you might want to use plain copier or printer paper, even though this kind of paper does not have much texture, or *tooth*. If you want your drawings to last a long time, use high-quality paper.

Terra-Cotta Pencil

Terra-cotta means "baked earth." Terra-cotta was a favorite drawing medium with artists like Michelangelo, perhaps because its warm color suggested the glow of human skin.

Magnificent Michelangelo

Already famous by the age of 15, Renaissance artist Michelangelo (1475–1564) is considered by many to be the greatest sculptor and painter of all time. Michelangelo was also highly skilled at drawing. His drawings were mostly of the human face and figure.

Prior to his death, Michelangelo burned a large number of his drawings and sketches (he did not want others to see works that he felt were not "perfect"), so the few that remain are quite valuable.

Michelangelo Buonarroti, *Study for the Head of Leda,* circa 1530. Red pencil, 354 x 269 mm. Gabinetto dei Disegni e delle Stampe, Uffizi, Florence, Italy.

White Art Eraser

Use for removing unwanted lines without smearing.

Smudger

Use the smudger to soften or blur your pencil lines.

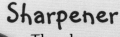

DID YOU KNOW?

Bending his head back for four years while painting the ceiling of the Sistine Chapel in Rome damaged Michelangelo's eyes—he had to hold letters over his head in order to read them.

Sharpener

The sharpener will work with all your pencils. Just be sure to hold it over a wastebasket when you sharpen!

The Secret Art Tool

And speaking of the wastebasket, many artists consider it an art tool as important as any other.

You will learn much more from your failures than from your successes. It is only by experience and with much practice that you can learn to draw what you envision, and even then, you may not get it right the first time.

The Basics

If you already hold your pencil this way, you just have to remember to hold it lightly.

Holding the Pencil

For all the drawing projects in this book, you will be using a pencil. Use this grip for most drawing that you do with the point of your pencil. Also, try to draw with your wrist and your whole arm sometimes, not just by moving your fingertips.

Hold your pencil like this when using the side of the lead. You will want to do this when shading and in many other kinds of drawing. It may feel funny to you at first, but try to get used to it.

Holding your pencil in a relaxed way will help you draw smooth, flowing lines. And your hand won't get so tired!

Not Like This

Above all, your grip should not look like this. A grip like this will make your fingers cramped and your lines tight and awkward.

Seeing Shapes

Much of art is learning how to see and draw basic shapes. Sharpen your medium pencil and copy this little drawing using plain paper.

This is a cube. A cube is a box with six sides, and each side is a square. But look how you have drawn it!

You drew it from a point of view that showed you three sides, and you used these shapes. None of your three shapes has the 90-degree angles of a square, and yet the object looks like a cube. This is because that is how a cube looks in *perspective*, or in three-dimensional space.

Drawing in Three Dimensions

All real objects have three dimensions: height, width, and depth. It is easy to show height and width in a drawing. Perspective helps your objects look like they have depth.

You can learn to draw a cube from any angle so that it still looks like a cube. Look at these examples and notice that while they all use different shapes, each one looks like a cube.

TRY IT!
Find an object that is cube-shaped or almost cube-shaped and is small enough to handle easily. Turn it around in your hands and watch how the different sides seem to change shape. Now try drawing it. See if you can do it so that each time it looks like the same object as seen from a different angle. The trick is to draw the sides as you actually see them (perhaps with short, slanted lines), not as you think they should be (perfect squares).

Beyond the Cube

Besides the cube, here are some other basic shapes to look for: the cone, the sphere, and the cylinder. Every object you see is based on one of these four shapes. You can find variations of these basic shapes in the drawings and paintings of most artists.

Sphere

Cylinder

Cone

How many different shapes can you find in Thiebaud's painting?

TIP It is a good idea to try to see basic shapes in everything you draw. Looking for basic shapes can help to simplify the scene in your mind.

Sweet Shapes

Wayne Thiebaud (born 1920) was especially interested in the strong, simple shapes he saw in his subjects. Thiebaud's luscious-looking images of carefully composed cakes and pies were called pop art.

Wayne Thiebaud, *Around the Cake*, 1962. Oil on canvas, 22 x 28 in. Spencer Museum of Art, Lawrence, Kansas.

Foreshortening for Depth

Take a close look at one of the basic shapes so you can learn something else you need to know: *foreshortening*. Even though objects stay the same size, your eyes and brain see parts of them as being shorter when viewed from certain angles. By changing the sizes of various items in a drawing, you can create the illusion of depth.

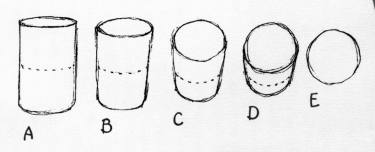

Here are some drawings of a cylinder. It has about the same proportions as a soda can, with a dotted line dividing it in half. You can see that as the cylinder tips toward you, the distance from the top rim to the bottom rim looks shorter and shorter, until at E it is completely hidden by the top surface. This is foreshortening, and it is very important in making convincing drawings.

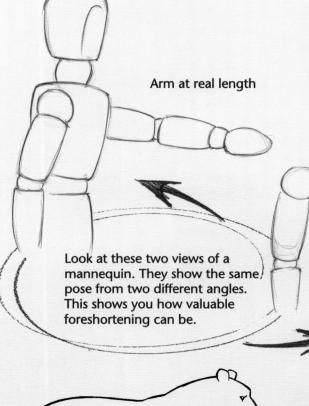

Arm at real length

Look at these two views of a mannequin. They show the same pose from two different angles. This shows you how valuable foreshortening can be.

Foreshortened arm

Look at the line drawn under the lion's feet. The legs that are farther away from you are drawn to be shorter so they don't touch the "floor." This gives the animal the appearance of depth.

Now look at this copy of an ancient Egyptian sculpture. Can you see what is interesting about it? There isn't any foreshortening! We don't know what their reasons were, but these great artists of long ago avoided foreshortening in their paintings and relief sculptures.

Bas-relief showing a pharaoh. Temple of Horus in Edfu.

Light and Shading

The objects we see around us are defined not only by their shapes, but also by their comparative lightness and darkness and by their color. Light and shading are important when drawing. You will learn about light and shade when you draw a still life.

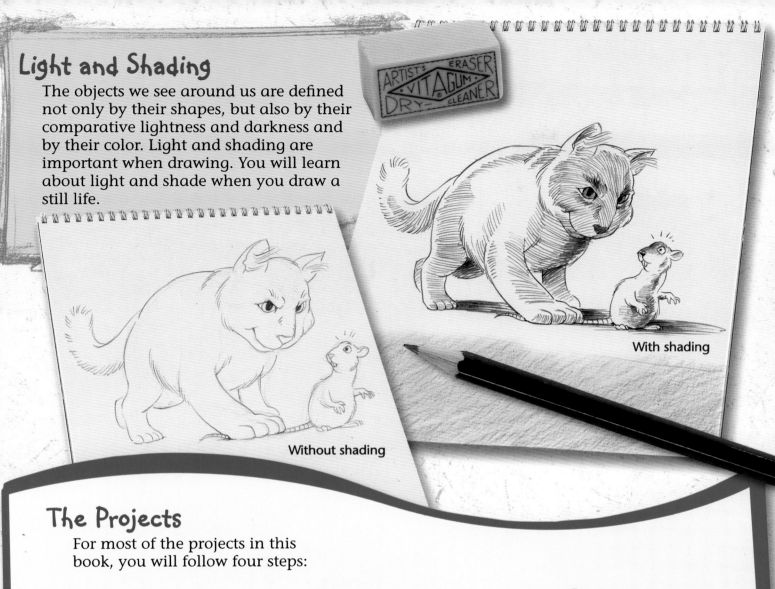

Without shading

With shading

The Projects

For most of the projects in this book, you will follow four steps:

① Block in the composition

② Draw the basic shapes

③ Add specific details

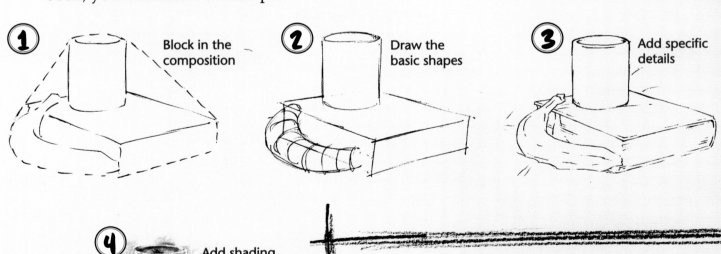

④ Add shading and highlights

About the Photographs

Because this is a book, you will be seeing photographs as examples to draw from. You can draw from your own photographs, too, but it is always best to draw from life—from real objects that are actually in front of you.

Still Life Drawing

A still life drawing is simply a picture of some objects in a small area.

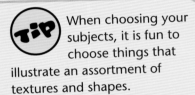

TIP When choosing your subjects, it is fun to choose things that illustrate an assortment of textures and shapes.

Light

With still life, you can work for many hours if you want, coming back to it again and again. Unless the objects you are drawing include perishable things, such as flowers or fruit, they will not change in appearance. But one thing that may change is your light. You should think about this if your drawing is going to take more than an hour.

Henri Matisse, *Still Life with Apples on a Pink Tablecloth*, 1924. Oil on canvas, 23¾ x 28¾ in. Chester Dale Collection, National Gallery of Art, Washington, D.C.

The Color of Joy

In this still life by Henri Matisse (1869–1954), the artist's interest in the lines and shapes of drawing is obvious. To Matisse, who studied law before he took up painting, creating art was a joyous activity and he wanted the viewer to share his pleasure. Matisse loved color and he worked to create art that could be understood by anyone. He said he wanted his colors to join in a living harmony, like a musical chord.

DID YOU KNOW?

Daylight changes constantly. After as little as one hour, the light may change enough to affect your drawing. If the sky becomes cloudy, the light may change completely and your shadows may disappear. And when the sun goes down, the electric lights you turn on will make your still life look completely different.

"Hatred, rancor, and the spirit of vengeance are useless baggage to the artist."

—Henri Matisse

Tips for Controlling Light

💡 Work fast. Plan your still life session so that you will have enough time in the right kind of light.

💡 Use artificial light only. If you do your drawing away from natural light, you can control your light at all times.

💡 Maybe you can take a reference photo to capture certain lighting conditions. If you have a Polaroid or digital camera, you can get an immediate photograph of the scene.

💡 When working outdoors, draw at the same time each day. This technique was used before the invention of photography. Painters wanting to capture a scene at sunset would only work on their painting at sunset each day.

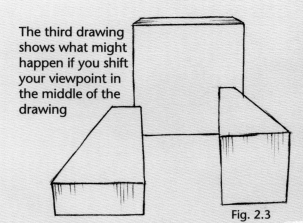

WATCH OUT!
If you start your drawing with your head in one place and then get up for a drink of water, watch out! If you are not paying attention, when you sit back down at your drawing the position of your eyes may be several inches to the right or left, or even above or below, where it was before.

Maintaining Your Point of View

The closer you are to your subject—to what you are drawing—the more important it is to keep the same point of view throughout the process. To keep your point of view from shifting, block in the main shapes right away. That is, quickly draw the position and basic shape of every item in the drawing. Don't work on any detail until you have done this, and try not to let yourself be interrupted during this process. The result is worth it.

Here you see examples of the same still life drawn from two slightly different points of view.

The third drawing shows what might happen if you shift your viewpoint in the middle of the drawing

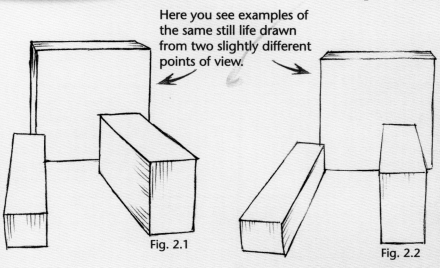

Fig. 2.1

Fig. 2.2

Fig. 2.3

Project: Still Life

Using familiar objects from your own house, assemble a still life to draw. Keep it simple for your first still life.

Here is a simple still life with just three objects:
- a book
- a cup
- a banana

Materials
- DRAWING PENCILS
- PLAIN PAPER

① Block In the Composition

First, block in all the main shapes and positions. That is, decide where the objects belong on your paper and what size or scale everything is to be.

Easier said than done! How do you decide those things? Here are a number of different ways you might place your still life arrangement on the paper.

Figure 2.4 shows everything at a distance. You are too far back from your subject, which not only makes the objects too small on the page, but it also leaves too much room all around the objects.

Fig. 2.4

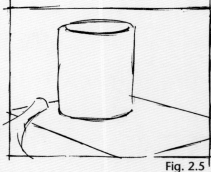

Figure 2.5 is closer, but perhaps now it is too close. You will have to leave out a lot of interesting detail, and you can't even see what the banana is!

Fig. 2.5

Figure 2.6 is better. It is a good size that leaves some breathing room around all your objects, while the objects themselves are large enough to be the center of attention.

Fig. 2.6

Working very lightly, use your 2H pencil for blocking in—you will want to erase some of these lines later.

Composition within the Frame

Now that you have decided on the size (scale), look at how the objects are positioned in the composition.

Sometimes artists compose pictures on purpose so that they are out of balance or somehow disturbing to look at, but you should have a reason for doing so.

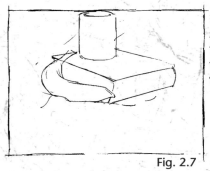

Fig. 2.7

Figure 2.7 has no space at the top; the cup is crowding the top edge of the frame.

Fig. 2.8

In figure 2.8, the corner of the book is actually touching the bottom of the frame. Both these compositions are uncomfortable because the eye cannot travel freely around the whole picture. Figure 2.6 is an example of a good basic composition, with enough space around the group of objects—yet not too much space.

Before You Start Drawing, Create the Boundaries of Your Composition

To block in the boundaries of your composition, try to see all the objects in your still life as a single object that has a shape. Imagine this shape in your mind and draw it on your paper. Here's how:

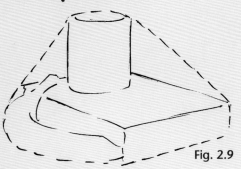

See the objects as one shape.

Fig. 2.9

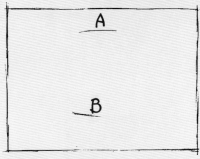

Imagine the shape only.

Fig. 2.10

Figure 2.10 is the same shape without any detail inside; it is the rough shape of all your objects clustered together.

Picture this shape fitting inside the area of your drawing paper.

Make a light horizontal mark near the top center of your page (A) to show where you want the top of your shape to be.

Make a mark near the bottom (B) where the point of the book comes down. You have located the top rim of the cup (A) and the bottom corner of the book (B).

Now, starting with the diagonal lines coming out from (B), carefully draw in the rest of the shape.

Like many things about drawing, this may take some practice.

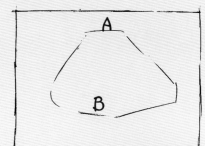

Mark the top and bottom boundaries of the shape.

Sketch the shape onto your paper.

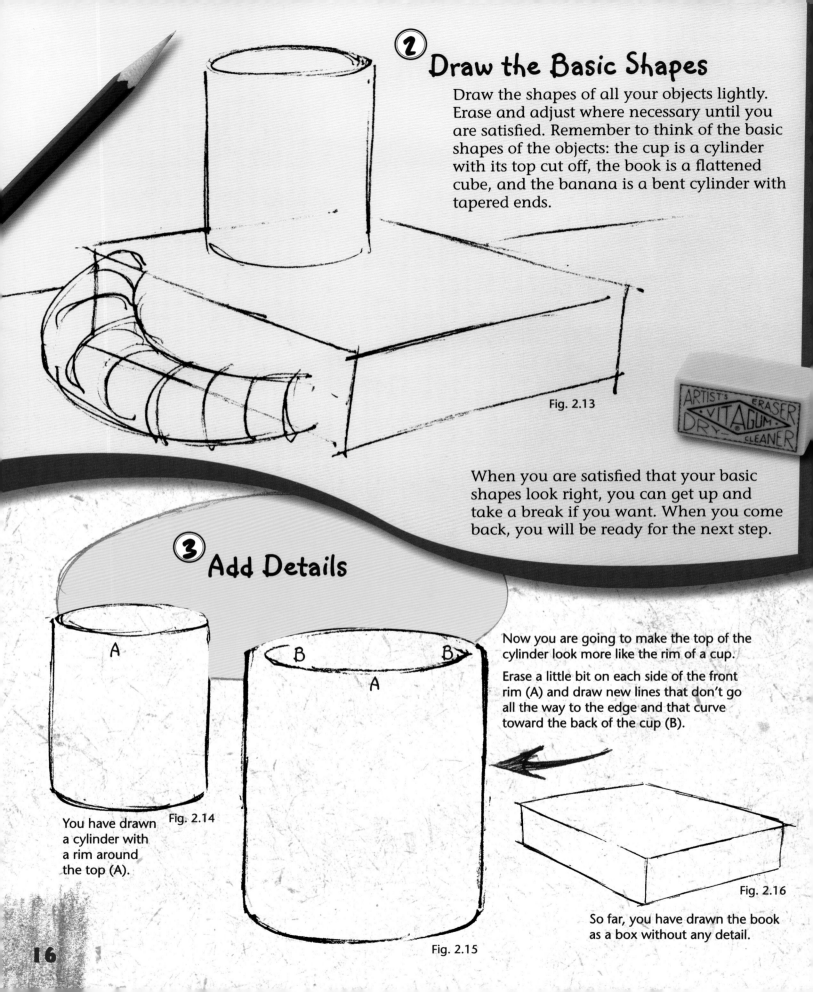

② Draw the Basic Shapes

Draw the shapes of all your objects lightly. Erase and adjust where necessary until you are satisfied. Remember to think of the basic shapes of the objects: the cup is a cylinder with its top cut off, the book is a flattened cube, and the banana is a bent cylinder with tapered ends.

Fig. 2.13

When you are satisfied that your basic shapes look right, you can get up and take a break if you want. When you come back, you will be ready for the next step.

③ Add Details

Now you are going to make the top of the cylinder look more like the rim of a cup.

Erase a little bit on each side of the front rim (A) and draw new lines that don't go all the way to the edge and that curve toward the back of the cup (B).

A

B B
A

You have drawn a cylinder with a rim around the top (A).

Fig. 2.14

Fig. 2.15

So far, you have drawn the book as a box without any detail.

Fig. 2.16

Even though parts of the book are hidden behind the cup (A) and the banana (B), think of the lines that make up the cube as being continuous (fig 2.17).

In figure 2.18, the thick covers of the book stick out a little from the stack of pages, and the pages are slightly curved (A). You can show some of the pages themselves with a series of lines that are parallel to the edges of the covers (B).

Fig. 2.17

Fig. 2.18

Side 4 only shows at the top.

You can follow sides 2 and 3 from the top of the banana to the bottom.

Side 1 appears only at the bottom.

The banana provides a good chance to practice foreshortening. Look at figure 2.13. Notice the lines that make the banana look as if it had been sliced crosswise into many pieces and put back together. You can lightly draw in similar lines (to be erased later) to help you follow the bending of the cylinder.

Fig. 2.19

Now all the main details are shown in your line drawing and you can go on to the shading.

TiP To keep from getting graphite on your hand and smearing it onto your drawing, place a clean piece of paper under your hand near the part of the drawing where you are working.

Fig. 2.20

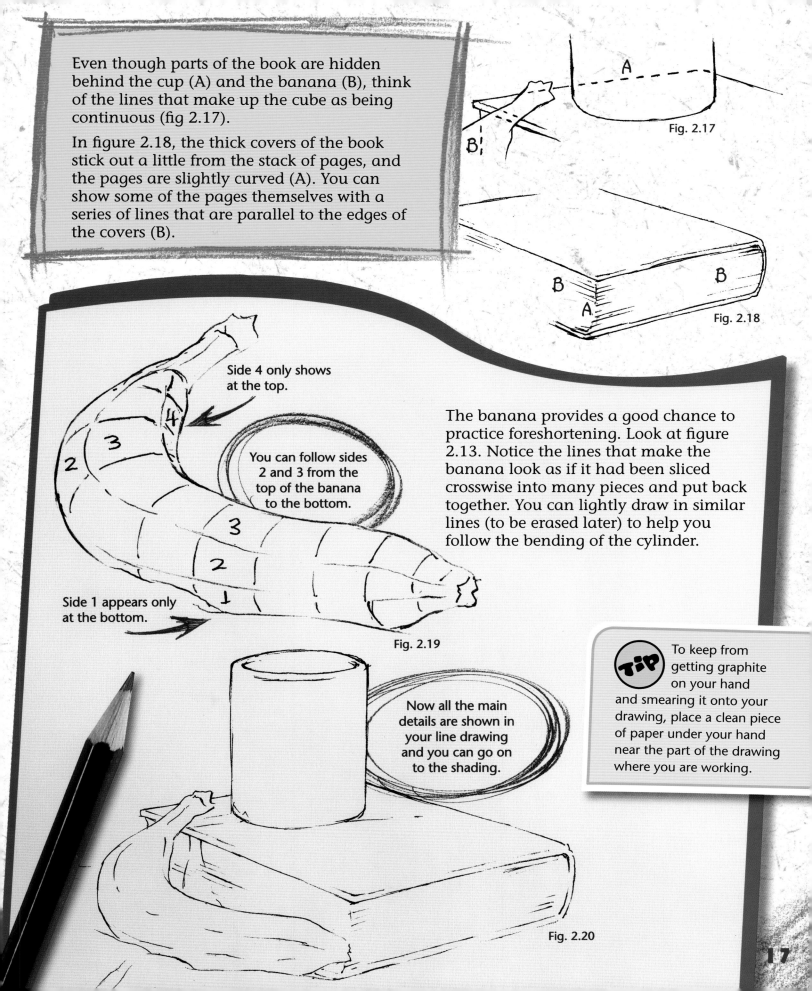

④ Shading

The line drawing you have made may show the shape and position of objects, but adding shading shows even more.

Light and Shadow

Now, as you are about to shade your drawing, you need to understand more about light and shadow. So, take a break from your still life and look at what's involved.

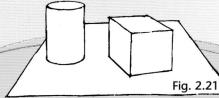

Fig. 2.21

Here you see a line drawing of a plain surface, like a square tabletop. On the surface are two basic shapes: a cylinder and a cube.

Now let's turn on a light, like a spotlight on the set of a movie.

Top Right

Top Left

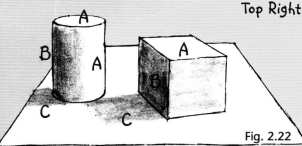

Fig. 2.22

The light is shining down from the upper right side, so the right sides and the tops of the objects are lit up (A). The sides away from the light are in shadow (B). Notice that the shading around the side of the cylinder is gradual, showing that it is a curved surface. Also, each object makes a cast shadow on the tabletop (C).

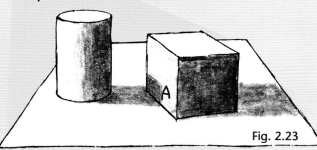

Fig. 2.23

Now the light source has moved to the other side. Notice that part of the shadow of the cylinder is cast onto the side of the cube (A).

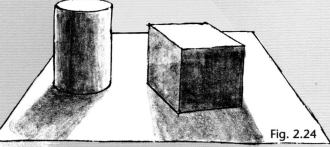

Back Light

Fig. 2.24

This shows light coming from the rear.

Straight Down

Fig. 2.25

This light shines straight down from the top.

All these lighting conditions are easy to understand—light on one side, darkness on the other side. But most of the lighting in real life is not that simple. Here are two examples:

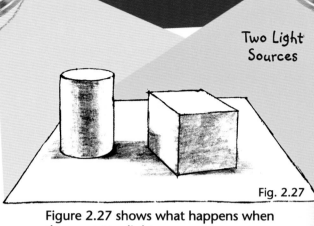

Two Light Sources

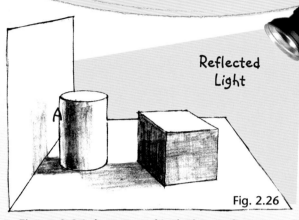

Reflected Light

Fig. 2.26

Figure 2.26 shows one kind of complication; it is just like figure 2.22 except that now we have added a new surface—a wall that is light colored and reflects the light back onto the dark area of the cylinder (A).

Fig. 2.27

Figure 2.27 shows what happens when there are two light sources at once.

Can you find this effect of reflected light in the room you are in right now?

LOTS OF LIGHT

In the real world, you will find this kind of lighting all the time. Sometimes there are more light sources than you can count! Some will be strong and some will be weak. Learn to look for shadows and reflections.

Now Return to Your Still Life

Look at the still life photo on page 14 again. Can you tell where the light or lights are coming from?

First of all, you can see that the banana is casting a dark shadow onto the side and top of the book and onto the cloth (A), so you know there is a light off to the left (B) that is making this happen.

The cup casts a shadow in the same direction onto the book, but it is lighter. Why? Because there is a second light! This light is shining from the right (C) and is strong enough to cancel out some of the shadows. It also strongly lights the right side of the cup (D) and the right edge of the book (E). The cover of the book is casting a strong shadow (F) onto the pages.

Fig. 2.28

Okay! Now you are ready to begin shading your still life!

19

Shade Large Areas First

Fill in the large areas first: the cover of the book, the main parts of the cup, and the shadow of the banana. Get them about as dark as you are going to want them so that you will be able to see the general shading of the whole drawing right away.

As you can see, the finished drawing is a combination of smoothly shaded areas (A) and roughly shaded areas (B).

Use the 4B pencil to do all your shading.

Fig. 2.29

TIP Use the side of your lead to shade large areas. It will blend better into a continuous tone and it is a faster way of working.

Styles of Shading

When shading with the pencil point, change direction several times (A). Doing this will gradually build up layers until you have the smoothness and darkness you want (B).

Shading with the side of the lead gives a different look (C).

After shading with the side of the lead, you can add a few detail marks on the top with the pencil point (D).

Still life drawings are fun to practice on rainy days!

Landscape Drawing

A landscape means just about anything you draw outdoors that includes a view into the distance. If you made a drawing showing a close view of a wagon wheel leaning against a barn, that would be more of a still life than a landscape.

Two similar classes of drawing are the seascape and the cityscape. But whether you are looking at a meadow, a body of water, or some buildings, the problems and solutions are generally the same.

Vincent van Gogh

This painting by the Dutch artist Vincent van Gogh (1853–1890) is a good example of a cityscape—a landscape that is all buildings and streets. Although now his work is loved the world over, the talented but troubled Van Gogh was never appreciated while he was alive. When he left paintings behind as he traveled, they were often destroyed or used to repair outbuildings. When he was desperately in need of money, he tried to sell his series of sunflower paintings for about $80. No one was interested. In 1987, one of his sunflower paintings sold for about $40 million.

Vincent van Gogh, *The Cafe Terrace on the Place du Forum, Arles, at Night*, 1888. Oil on canvas, 65.5 x 81.0 cm. Rijksmuseum Kroeller-Mueller, Otterlo, The Netherlands.

"There are two ways to thinking about painting, how not to do it and how to do it: how to do it-with much drawing and little color; how not to do it-with much color and little drawing."
—Vincent van Gogh

Light and Wind

The one important thing you must always deal with when drawing a landscape is weather. With landscape, the light is always natural light—some kind of sunlight. You may have to deal with light that changes in moments from strong sunlight to muted light coming through clouds. This could be a problem.

Van Gogh once made himself a lilac-colored suit with yellow spots on it.

Suppose you were drawing something with strong shadows?

If the sun went behind a cloud, you would suddenly have lower contrast and the whole picture could change.

And then there is wind. A breeze you might not even notice while taking a walk or playing ball can be quite annoying if it is ruffling the pages of your sketchbook while you are trying to work.

Composing Your Landscape

As with every drawing, you must first pick your subject and decide on the composition. With a landscape, you need to make a decision about where to place the *horizon line*. The horizon is where the land or water meets the sky, especially where it is flat, like on an ocean or in a desert.

The Horizon Line

Here is a little house in a field with trees at the back and buildings at both sides.

Van Gogh's composition leads your eye from the beach right out to the horizon line.

Vincent van Gogh, *Fishing Boats on the Beach at Saintes-Maries*, 1888. Oil on canvas, 65.0 x 81.5 cm. Van Gogh Museum, Amsterdam, The Netherlands.

If you want to leave out the other buildings, try a closer view of the house.

If you move out a little more you can show some sky (A) and the horizon (B) while still not showing the buildings.

You can also place the horizon higher.

Or you can place the horizon line lower.

You will have to experiment to find the composition that is best for your drawing.

Project: Landscape

Working outdoors, if possible, draw a landscape that includes something in the far distance, something near to you, and something halfway in between.

Materials
- DRAWING PENCILS
- PLAIN PAPER
- DRAWING SURFACE, CLIPBOARD, OR EASEL

Here is a little pioneer house preserved in a park. It has a simple shape and a weathered look that will be fun to draw.

① Block In the Composition

Using your hard pencil, lightly block in the outlines of the house, the big tree in front, and the light pole. Lightly draw in the location of the sidewalk in front of the house and the horizon line.

The horizon line is about in the middle of the house (notice where the white tree trunks in the back touch the ground).

② Identify the Main Shapes

The house is a cube with lots of rectangles on it. The light pole and tree trunk are long, skinny cylinders. The light fixture, the bushes, and the outline of the tree leaves are spheres.

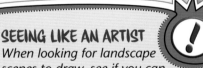

SEEING LIKE AN ARTIST
When looking for landscape scenes to draw, see if you can find a scene that has both horizontal (side to side) and vertical (up and down) lines and shapes. This makes your drawing more interesting.

This may be a pretty scene, but it is not very interesting.

Try shifting your point of view to show the vertical lines of the trees and the fence cutting into the horizontal lines. Much better!

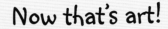

Now that's art!

❸ Add Details

Now you are ready to add detail. Don't be put off if something looks too complicated! There is usually a way to turn complex things into simple patterns that will tell the story. The shingles on the roof of this little house are a good example.

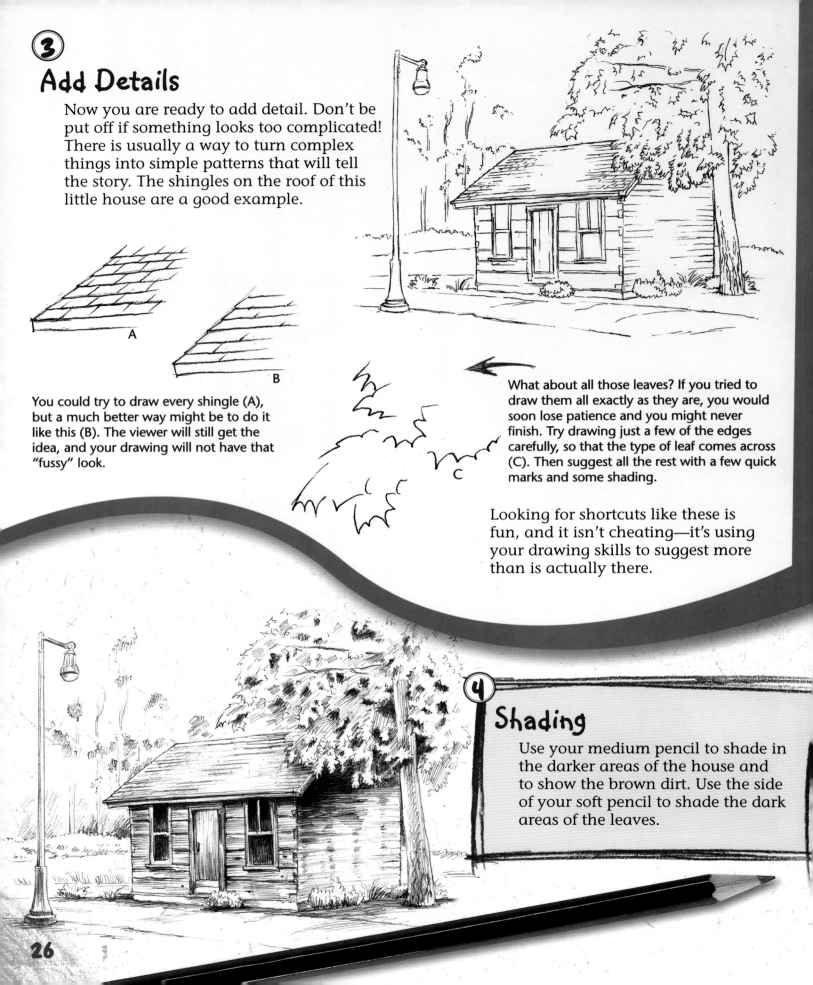

A

B

You could try to draw every shingle (A), but a much better way might be to do it like this (B). The viewer will still get the idea, and your drawing will not have that "fussy" look.

C

What about all those leaves? If you tried to draw them all exactly as they are, you would soon lose patience and you might never finish. Try drawing just a few of the edges carefully, so that the type of leaf comes across (C). Then suggest all the rest with a few quick marks and some shading.

Looking for shortcuts like these is fun, and it isn't cheating—it's using your drawing skills to suggest more than is actually there.

❹ Shading

Use your medium pencil to shade in the darker areas of the house and to show the brown dirt. Use the side of your soft pencil to shade the dark areas of the leaves.

Fabulous!

Even though we are leaving out some details, such as the pipe on the side of the house, all the important information is there.

From now on, every time you go outside, you will be looking at the world through the eyes of an artist!

TIP If you take your sketchbook and a few pencils with you every time you leave the house, you can practice landscapes any time you want!

Portrait Drawing

Portrait drawing is a kind of figure drawing—a drawing in which a human is the focus. In a portrait, there is a lot of emphasis on the face and the likeness—whether it looks like the person you are drawing or not. But the portrait can be a lot more than that, too. Body language—how a person naturally sits or stands—can contribute almost as much to the likeness as the face does.

Chances are you have already tried drawing a portrait before, so you know how hard it can be—and part of the reason is that your subject is alive.

It isn't natural for living creatures to hold completely still. Even a dog lying down may not hold still for as long as you hope.

Romantic Rossetti

As a painter, a poet, and a man, Dante Gabriel Rossetti (1828–1882) was a Romantic with a capital *R*. Rossetti co-founded the Pre-Raphaelite Brotherhood, a group of English poets and painters who wanted to revive the richness and idealized beauty of the medieval period. The Pre-Raphaelites were part of an artistic movement called Romanticism, which stressed romantic love, strong emotion, and imagination. He was married to one of his most beautiful models.

Dante Gabriel Rossetti, *La Ghirlandata*, 1873. Guildhall Art Gallery, London, Great Britain.

There are so many types of faces with so many combinations of features that it would take a whole book just to show a fraction of the possibilities. Just look at the differences in these seven faces alone!

"Her voice was like the voice the stars had when they sang together."
—Dante Gabriel Rossetti

Tips for Drawing Faces

Even though every face is different, here is one system that some artists use to draw a realistic-looking head.

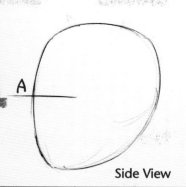

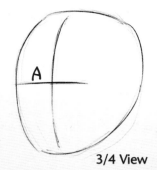

Think of the head as a big oval shape. Here you see the side view and the three-quarter view of an oval head.

A line (A) halfway down marks the center of the eyes.

Side View

3/4 View

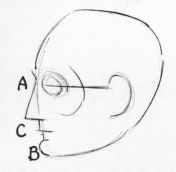

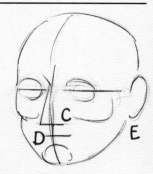

Halfway between the center of the eyes (A) and the tip of the chin (B) is the bottom of the nose (C).

The mouth (D) is about halfway between the bottom of the nose and the tip of the chin. Line up the corners of the mouth with the eye centers.

The bottom of the ear (E) is as far down as the bottom of the nose, or slightly lower, and the ear is about the same length as the nose.

Once you have sketched the basic features in their positions, add details.

Last, add the remaining details that make up the individual face: the hair, eyebrows, and other features that combine to make each person unique.

Drawing Children

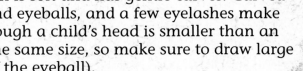

On a child's face, the forehead takes up much more space than it does on an adult's face, so the eyes will be below the halfway line. A child's nose is often rounded on the sides and the top, and the mouth is soft and has gentle curves. Curved eyelids frame the round eyeballs, and a few eyelashes make the eyes look real. Though a child's head is smaller than an adult's, the eyes are the same size, so make sure to draw large irises (the dark part of the eyeball).

29

Project: Portrait of a Child

This project will be a drawing of a photo of a little boy. Since small children cannot hold still at all, a photo may be the best way to get a child to be your model.

Materials
- TERRA-COTTA PENCIL
- WHITE PENCIL
- COLORED PAPER

NOTE:
You might want to practice this section on plain paper with graphite pencils before trying it with your terra-cotta pencil and good-quality paper.

Children are in some ways harder—and in some ways easier—to draw than grown-ups. Children's faces don't have a lot of creases, wrinkles, and hard edges—lines an artist can use to divide the face into convenient sections. On the other hand, those details can distract you from the basics, which is all you have in the face of a child.

You begin with the shape of the head and the shape of the face, and then you just have to put the features—eyes, brows, nose, mouth, and ears—in the right places.

To keep it simple, let's leave out the high chair and the child's hand.

① Draw the Basic Shapes

One way to get the oval of the head right is to draw a very faint circle (A). Lightly draw a line across the middle of the circle (B).

Starting at this middle line, draw a second circle just like the first one (C). Then draw a faint line down the middle of these two circles (D).

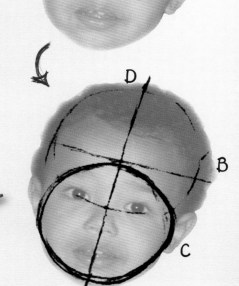

② Mark Where the Features Will Go

Now draw a faint line across the area where the two circles intersect (E). This is the centerline of the eyes. Make a mark halfway between the eye line and the chin (F); this shows where the bottom of the nose will be.

Make a mark halfway between the nose line and the chin (G). This is the location of the mouth.

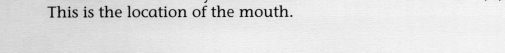

③ Add Details

Now that you know where the features will go, lightly draw in their shapes. Keep looking back at the photograph (or at your model) to get the right distance between the eyes, and between the eyebrows and the hairline. In most people, eyebrows start and end with the corners of the eyes.

Work to get the basic head shape right.

Add the ears, chin, hair, and neck, but don't worry about shading yet. Draw the lines lightly. Erase lines as needed.

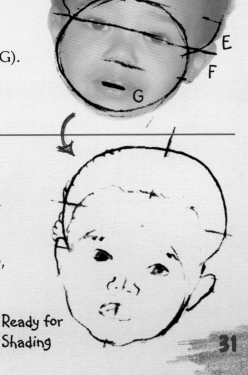

Ready for Shading

31

④ Add Shading and Highlighting

When shading and highlighting a drawing, think in terms of three tones: dark, middle, and light. Because you have used a medium-colored paper for your portrait drawing, the paper will serve as the middle tone. Now all you need to do is add the dark and light areas.

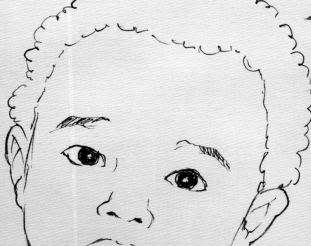

You can practice shading on this drawing first.

Shade the Edges and Curves

Look at the lines on the drawing that define edges and curves: the shape of the head and the outlined curves of the nose, lips, ears, and eyes. Lightly shade these areas and watch how the face gets a more rounded shape as the shaded areas "move back."

Highlight the Areas of Reflected Light

Now look at the photograph to see where the light is reflected: the eyes, the tip of the nose, the top of the bottom lip, and the teeth. Use the white pencil to add a small touch of white to these areas. Use the eraser to remove color from areas that you have made too dark.

Here is a handy way to think about what to shade and what to highlight:

Dark areas:
- Appear to recede, or move back
- Define edges of things
- Show where a surface curves

Light areas:
- Appear to come forward
- Show reflected light
- Show where surfaces peak (like the tip of the nose and the area under the eyebrows)

Other Approaches to Portraits

When Symphony in White, No. 1 *was first displayed, art critics searched for meaning in the girl's pose and face. They said she was a sleepwalker or a ghost. In fact, Whistler had deliberately told the model to gaze vacantly and let her arms hang loose so that people would see only the beauty of the painting without attaching any meaning to it. Whistler called this "art for art's sake."*

Whistler

James McNeill Whistler (1834–1903) believed that art did not need to have any other purpose than to be beautiful. That is why his subjects are often just standing (or sitting) still.

James McNeill Whistler, *Symphony in White, No. 1: The White Girl,* 1862. Oil on canvas. Harris Whittemore Collection, National Gallery of Art, Washington, D.C.

Oh Baby!

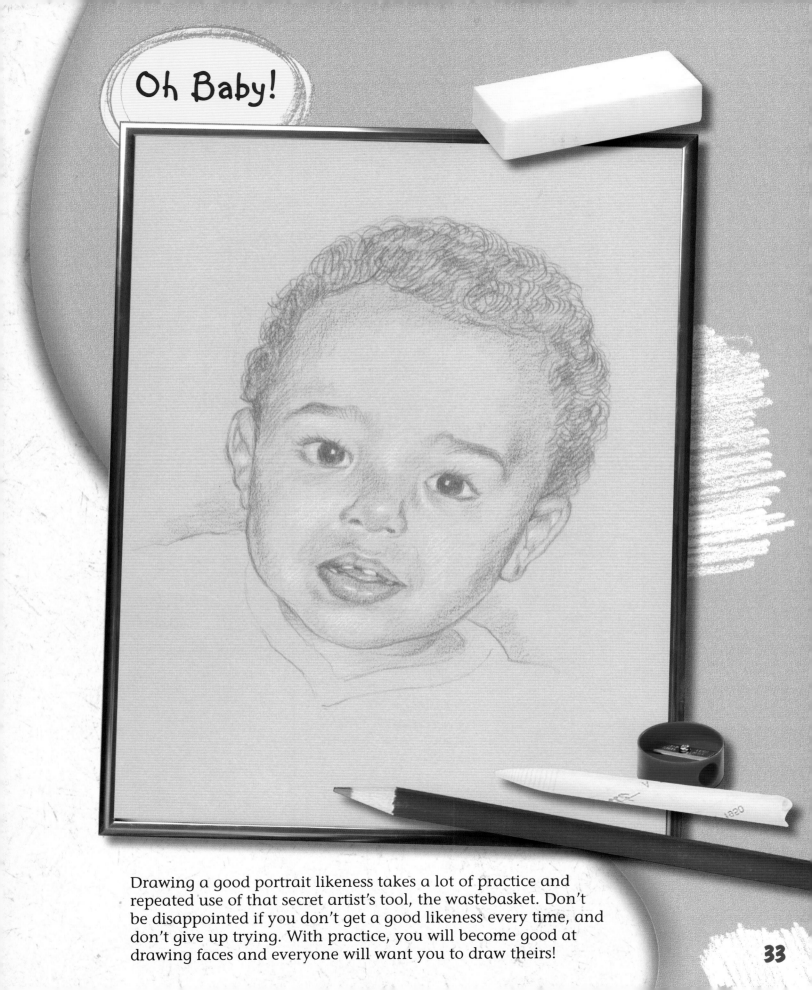

Drawing a good portrait likeness takes a lot of practice and repeated use of that secret artist's tool, the wastebasket. Don't be disappointed if you don't get a good likeness every time, and don't give up trying. With practice, you will become good at drawing faces and everyone will want you to draw theirs!

Imaginative Drawing

You know something about this kind of drawing already—it is how every artist starts out. From your imagination, you can draw creatures, places, and things that no one has ever seen before. It is fun to do, and perhaps best of all, nobody can point at your drawing and say, "That doesn't look right." Your drawing of a fairy, your sketch of a futuristic city, or your cartoon of a mouse that walks on its hind feet and wears pants—these things are from your imagination.

"People love mystery, and that is why they love my paintings."
—Salvador Dalí

Salvador Dalí, *The Persistence of Memory*, 1931. Oil on canvas, 9½ x 13 in. © The Museum of Modern Art / Licensed by Scala/Art Resource, NY.

Salvador Dalí's life was as creative and offbeat as his paintings. He wore a long, thin mustache that was waxed on the ends so it pointed toward the sky, he had a stuffed polar bear to hold umbrellas, and he once drove around in a Rolls Royce filled with cauliflower.

When critics accused him of going too far, Dalí replied, "It's the only place I ever wanted to go."

Salvador Dalí

The surrealist painter Salvador Dalí (1904–1989) often created strange landscapes filled with fantastic creatures and objects. Even the imaginative objects in Dalí's paintings appeared solid and real because of his skill in depicting light, shapes, and surfaces.

Dalí

One night, instead of going to the movies with friends, Dalí sat at the dinner table staring at melting Camembert cheese. Before going to bed that night, he added three melting watches to a landscape he was painting. This landscape became *The Persistence of Memory*, possibly his most famous painting.

Drawing from Imagination Tips

Here are some pointers on how to get the best results when you try to draw what you are imagining.

① Draw Your Character in Situations

If you have a character that you have invented, you may enjoy drawing that character over and over again. But instead of drawing him "just standing there," it is much more effective to show him doing something.

This drawing shows a little man in a suit just standing there. He may look interesting, but you don't understand much about him with such a pose.

Here the same little man is studying something on a piece of paper, and he is obviously unhappy about it. It makes a more interesting drawing in every way, and it gives you a chance to try out your acting skills with your characters.

TiP When working with the mannequin, it isn't necessary to draw all the ball joints or the exact shape of the parts. Just get the pose.

② For Character Poses, Use Your Mannequin

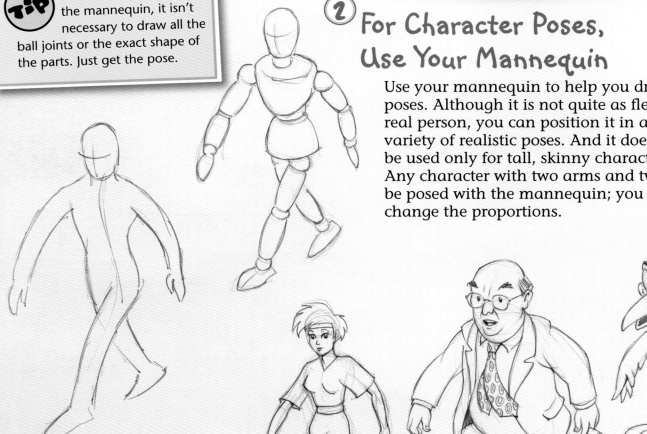

Use your mannequin to help you draw character poses. Although it is not quite as flexible as a real person, you can position it in an amazing variety of realistic poses. And it doesn't have to be used only for tall, skinny characters, either. Any character with two arms and two legs can be posed with the mannequin; you just have to change the proportions.

Using the same pose every time, you can create drawings of characters with very different body types—for example, an anime-style girl, a businessman, and a cartoon bird. You can see that they are all based on the same pose, but for some the arms and legs are shorter or longer.

Notice how foreshortening was used on the right leg in each case.

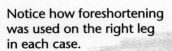

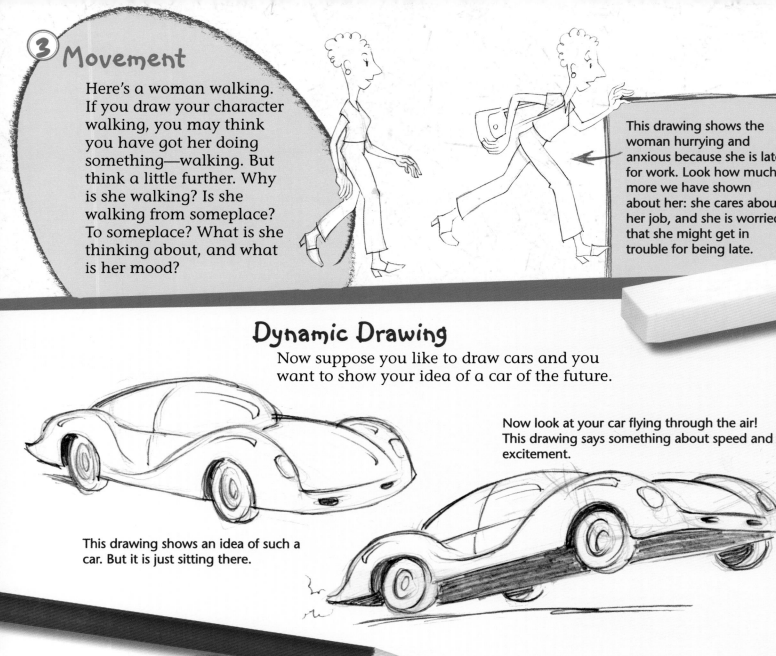

③ Movement

Here's a woman walking. If you draw your character walking, you may think you have got her doing something—walking. But think a little further. Why is she walking? Is she walking from someplace? To someplace? What is she thinking about, and what is her mood?

This drawing shows the woman hurrying and anxious because she is late for work. Look how much more we have shown about her: she cares about her job, and she is worried that she might get in trouble for being late.

Dynamic Drawing

Now suppose you like to draw cars and you want to show your idea of a car of the future.

This drawing shows an idea of such a car. But it is just sitting there.

Now look at your car flying through the air! This drawing says something about speed and excitement.

Animators often draw roughly in red or blue pencil, then "clean up" the drawing with bold, deliberate strokes of a dark graphite pencil, without erasing the colored lines at all. This started in the days when animation drawings were traced onto plastic sheets by hand. The black pencil line became the only line that mattered, and it was easy to ignore the red or blue lines without erasing them. Try it yourself!

④ Research

Looking at a few pictures from a book or on the Internet can help you draw all kinds of things, like this cartoon view of big city skyscrapers.

Artist's Face in the Mirror

Here is the artist's expression on three very different faces. (Note: When doing this, it is not necessary to make a drawing of yourself first; just put the expression straight onto your character.)

TIP For expressions, try looking in a mirror. Drawing your characters with good facial expressions adds a lot to your drawings, and there's one model who's always available to make faces for you—yourself! Many artists use a small shaving mirror that is attached to their drawing board, but you can use a mirror in your bathroom or anywhere else.

Project: Fantasy Drawing

Using reference from reality, make a fantasy drawing as real as you can.

Let's say, for example, you want to draw a picture of a little fairy. Perhaps you have an image in your mind, and you could just draw it. It might look something like this.

It looks fine just as it is. But suppose you wanted it to be a bit more convincing. What could you do? You could look at other artists' drawings of fairies, but you want it to be your own. Instead, you could think about it like this: your fairy is, basically, a pretty little girl hovering in the air, and she has the wings of a butterfly.

In order to make her more convincing, how about looking for some pictures of the things that make up your fairy: a pretty girl's face, a pose like someone hovering in the air, and some butterfly wings. For these things, you could look in books, magazines, or maybe on the Internet.

Materials
- TERRA-COTTA PENCIL
- WHITE PENCIL
- COLORED PAPER

TiP To make fantasy believable, base it on reality.

Here Are Some Examples from Various Sources

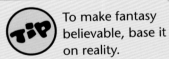

For a good face, how about some clothing ads showing smiling girls of the right age?

For the pose, you might find a good photograph, but you could also look at yourself in the mirror, or try posing your mannequin.

As for butterfly wings, a book on insects or a butterfly Web site should be easy to find.

Beautiful!

When you put them all together, you get a very different image than the first one you drew. Is it any better? That's up to you, but you have learned a good way of getting a different look if you are unhappy with your first try.

Something else has happened, too. Because you have done the drawing twice, you have simply put a lot more thought into it the second time. Sometimes just drawing something over is enough to improve it!

Give Your Character an Environment

Because a fairy might be found in a garden, why not draw some flowers beneath your fairy, as though she is about to touch them with her wand? You can draw the flowers from your imagination, or you can find some good flower pictures to help you make them realistic.

But however you do it, drawing from imagination is always fun.

Drawing from History

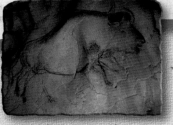

30,000 YEARS AGO
Over 30,000 years ago, the earliest humans decorated the walls of caves with pictures of bison, horses, deer, and mammoths.

Do you think Stone Age humans drew multiple legs on this bison to make it look as though it were running?

Bas-relief showing a pharaoh. Temple of Horus in Edfu.

3000–1000 BC
When it came to drawing on walls, no one did more of it than the ancient Egyptians.

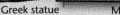
Greek statue

Michelangelo, *Study for the Head of Leda*, circa 1530.

1400–1600
The artwork of the Egyptians influenced the ancient Greeks, who were the inspiration for much of the art of the European Renaissance.

These artists were sometimes called Fauves (FOVES), a French word meaning "wild beasts."

Henri Matisse, *Still Life with Apples on a Pink Tablecloth,* 1924. © Succession H. Matisse, Paris/ARS

Vincent van Gogh, *Fishing Boats on the Beach at Saintes-Maries*, 1888.

1800S
After several centuries of realistically drawing "important things," artists in the late 1800s began to paint and draw places and things that were important just to them.

Salvador Dalí, *The Persistence of Memory*, 1931. © The Museum of Modern Art.

20TH CENTURY
As the twentieth century progressed, artists pushed the limits of art even further. *Surrealist* (beyond realism) artists, like Salvador Dalí, explored the unconscious mind with paintings they called "dreamscapes."

Pop artists, on the other hand, painted everyday objects, challenging the viewer to think of the objects in a new way.

Wayne Thiebaud, *Around the Cake*, 1962.

EARLY 1900S
After World War I (1914–1918), some artists returned to the strong outlines and two-dimensional flatness used in cave drawing and early Greek art.

If you approach each new drawing as an adventure, you will never lose your love for the fine art—and the fun—of drawing.

Today, artists have the freedom to draw whatever is in their imagination. Who knows, maybe the next important art movement will be started by YOU!